# Empowering Women
## THROUGH THE STORM

# *Empowering Women*
## THROUGH THE STORM

### The Trials and Tribulations of Life

FORLANDA ANDERSON

*Empowering Women through the Storm: The Trials and Tribulations of Life*

© 2017 Forlanda Anderson

All rights reserved. No part of this book may be reproduced in any written, electronic, recording, or photocopying without written permission of the publisher or author. The exception would be in the case of brief quotations embodied in the critical articles or reviews and pages where permission is specifically granted by the publisher or author.

Most scriptures taken from the Holy Bible, New International Version®, NIV®. Copyright © 1973, 1978, 1984, 2011 by Biblica, Inc.™ Used by permission of Zondervan. All rights reserved worldwide. www.zondervan.com The "NIV" and "New International Version" are trademarks registered in the United States Patent and Trademark Office by Biblica, Inc.™

ISBN 978-1-4956-2015-7 (paperback)
ISBN 978-1-4956-2016-4 (epub)
ISBN 978-1-4956-2017-1 (mobi)

Printed in the United States of America

# Contents

| | |
|---|---|
| Acknowledgments | vii |
| Introduction | 1 |
| Seven Principles to Remember before the Storm | 3 |
| Daily Affirmations for Women | 11 |
| Power of a Woman | 17 |
| The Storm | 25 |
| Knowing Who You Are | 33 |
| Accountability Partners | 39 |
| Role Models | 49 |
| What Is Your Chapter Called? | 63 |
| Empowering Women with Love | 77 |
| Key Points to Take Away | 83 |
| Resources to Help You Face Your Storm | 87 |
| About the Author | 95 |
| Prayers | 97 |
| Answered Prayers | 101 |
| Notes | 103 |

*Acknowledgments*

Growing up, as a little girl, I would always see my peers comparing themselves to others and competing with one another. Watching them think less of themselves because they were different or didn't have everything that the girls on television did had become the norm.

As I grew older, I knew that wasn't the way life was supposed to be. Both of my parents taught me not only to be thankful for what I had but also to never look down on those who were less fortunate.

My parents taught me what it meant to be humble and to love myself, as well as others. They taught me to keep God first in anything and everything that I do. Now I can attest that everything I learned as a child molded me into the woman

I am today. Without the help of two strong individuals who made it a point to teach me how important the little things in life were, I wouldn't know the true meaning of *empowering women*.

This book is dedicated to my two parents and all the beautiful women with beautiful souls who were created to make a difference in the world. To all the fierce women who live in the confidence of the skin that they are in. You all are phenomenal. You are special. You are life.

# Introduction

/Storm\—(n.) A serious disturbance of any element of nature.

As women, we all experience storms in our journey of life, no matter if it is a mild storm, a heavy storm, or a tsunami. Storms can come at any time and on any day.

> They do not discriminate or reside
> in a precise location.

It doesn't matter if your day is as bright as the sun that shines from above or as gloomy as a starless night; a storm can accumulate right in your backyard. In other words, no matter where you are in life, something unexpected can occur and change your entire world.

That is why it is important for women to help each other in times when the storms arise. Whether you are ten or a hundred, you are never too young or too old to experience a storm.

That also goes for empowering your fellow sister: no one is too young or too old to lend a helping hand to another woman when she is having a bad day, a bad year, or even a bad life. It is important to realize the power that women possess.

When women come together and help each other, we become so powerful that nothing and no one can stop us.

We become—

Magic.

# Seven Principles to Remember before the Storm

Life can be tricky at times. It is like a game with basic instructions to a puzzle that you must put together by searching the world for the missing pieces. Sometimes storms will arise and destroy the pieces that you've worked so hard to obtain. But when your feet are planted in God's word, you'll have every answer on how to recover the pieces that were destroyed within the storm. Following these key principles will assist you in not only finding the pieces to your puzzle but making it out of the storm with power and dignity. Before the storm, it is important that your mind is in the right place. Know that if everything in your life has been going wonderfully for so long, a storm is scheduled to knock on your door sooner or later.

**Principle 1: Mind-set/affirmations.** Going into a storm with the right mind-set will increase the probability of making it out of the storm stronger than you were before. If you face a storm head-on with a weak mind-set, then that is a setup for disaster. You're telling yourself that the storms you face will defeat you before they even arrive. Instead, tell yourself how strong you are, how intelligent you are, and how powerful you are. What you think is what you tell yourself, and what you tell yourself will determine your actions. Be mindful of what consumes your thoughts. Those thoughts will control your life. Contribute positive thoughts to your mind and you will begin to see positive results in your life. This goes for helping others as well as helping yourself get through tough storms. When it comes to helping others, do so with the right mind-set: not to get anything in return but to help others from the kindness of your heart and for the simple fact that they are in need of help.

**Principle 2: Power.** Storms aren't always easy to get through, but because of the power God has placed within you, you'll have enough strength to endure until the end. You have the power to overcome anything that comes before you; you just have to realize it and know when to use it. The power you possess is internal and can be reflected on the outside when used correctly. You have strength both mentally and physically to fight through some of the hardest and toughest storms. Keep in mind that God knows how much you are able to handle. He gives his toughest battles to his strongest soldiers. So if you have been experiencing difficult trials and tribulations, it is because God knows you are strong enough to handle it. Keep going and don't get discouraged.

**Principle 3: Know yourself.** You must know who you are before going into the storm; otherwise, you'll get lost within it. Know who you are so that no matter the severity of the tests and trials that come your way, you won't allow them to change you into something you're not. This is an essential life skill that everyone should obtain. This will allow you to not be moved and to remain whole.

**Principle 4: Accountability partners.** Have an accountability partner for support during times when you feel your weakest—times when you need someone to depend on, to help you stay above water in life. Someone who is trustworthy and will help correct you when you are wrong. This is a person who coaches you to complete and accomplish various tasks within your life. An accountability partner is an important person to keep in your corner when facing a tough storm.

**Principle 5: Role models**. A role model serves as a positive influence for others to look up to. Children in this day and time are in desperate need of influential role models and guidance. Be a good role model to help the younger generation so that they'll know what to do when storms arise in their lives and so that they can grow to be a generation of strong women with power and dignity.

**Principle 6: Prayer**. Prayer can be your best friend if you let it. Prayer changes things, and having a prayer plan and executing it every chance you get will be the difference between experiencing the normal and the supernatural. Prayer can help eliminate worry and anxiety, open doors of opportunity, and help prevent bad decisions. It can also get you through any storm that appears to be coming your way. There's power in prayer.

**Principle 7: Love.** When empowering women through the storms of life, do so with a genuine and loving heart. Love will take you to places you never imagined you'd go. Loving yourself, loving your enemies, and loving others even in times when it may be difficult is the master key to unlocking doors.

These key principles will not only help you make it through the tests, trials, and storms that life comes with, but they will also show you that you can help uplift other women along the way. **Life is about empowering each other and helping one another while trying to live your best life and be the best you that you can be despite the circumstances and storms that may come your way.**

There are so many different types of storms: physical, mental, emotional, medical, financial, and the list goes on and on. We must know what to do when these storms arise. We must not lose our minds but use our minds to make it through. Some storms are seen, but most are unseen. They are usually, but not always, internal and invisible.

Women are able to hide things so well that others may never know that we are going through a storm. The entire world could be crashing down, but we'll still be walking around with smiles on our faces. We may have more bills than money, but guess what? No one may ever know.

You might look like you have everything together and have the perfect life. You could even have other women envy you or become jealous of what it looks like you have. But little do they know, nothing has been going right for you. On the outside, they could see a happy relationship or marriage, but in reality, you could be crying yourself to sleep every night. They could be jealous of you for taking that new job, but you dread going every single day.

That woman you see with the perfect body, perfect car, perfect career, and perfect life that you consider "goals" may be the very woman that is completely unhappy with her life. Everything you consider to be perfection could very well be a disaster in reality. Storms aren't always clear or noticeable for many people who are on the outside looking in.

So before you begin to compare yourself to others, consider the storms they may have had to endure or the storms they are currently facing that you are unaware of. You must know that every single person living on earth will experience or has experienced some type of storm. Some women have experienced minor storms, and others have experienced severe storms that were meant to destroy them. Some women have experienced damaging storms, life-changing storms. But you know the good thing about those intense storms? The women who faced them made it through.

Storms are made to destroy, disturb, and move things around. Which means your life can change in a matter of seconds. Anything can happen at any time of your life. Each day we wake up, we never know what we'll be faced with. No one knows when a storm will occur, and no one knows your future except God.

Therefore, you have to put on the right armor and be willing to let God walk before you. No matter what life hits you with, by all means, you have to keep going.

## Daily Affirmations for Women

>Let God transform you into a new person
>by changing the way you think.
>
>—Romans 12:2

You are enough.
You are beautiful in your own skin.
You are smart.
You are strong.
You are powerful.
You are special.
You are worthy.
You can do anything you put your mind to.
Always think positive.
Pray through the good and the bad.
Walk in confidence.
Feed your mind, body, and soul daily.
Love yourself.
Be yourself.
By all means, *never. give. up*!

> And remember, no one can be you . . . better than you can.

Remembering these daily affirmations as a woman can strengthen your mind in a positive way. What you tell yourself is very important. Whatever you allow to consume your thoughts will control your life. Your mindset will determine the type of day you have. If you wake up and focus your mind on something negative that happened the night before, then guess what? You probably won't have a good day. But if you focus your thoughts on the brand-new day ahead of you and all the possibilities and ways you can make today better than yesterday, then you are likely to have a much more pleasant day.

Not only can the way you think change the way you feel, the way you live, or the way your day is going, but it can change your life. Opening your mind to new things is sometimes a good idea. Whether it is starting a new hobby, learning about a new culture, or even traveling to see new places, it is healthy to step outside of your comfort zone sometimes—especially if it involves helping others.

Nowadays, it is almost rare to see women helping one another. In these times, it is crucial that we as women lend a helping hand to the next woman. Even if it is just complimenting your fellow sister, you will never know how much that one compliment may have boosted her confidence or made her feel better about herself. On several occasions, I can remember coming across young girls and women who would blatantly talk about the next woman after noticing something unappealing—for example, something wrong with her hair, or tissue stuck under her shoe, or that her backpack was unzipped. Instead of talking to her or helping her, they would just laugh and continue on about their day, not realizing that sometimes, God puts us in certain places at certain times for a certain purpose. You could be the only person that God sent to help someone. Recognizing that and taking advantage of it will help you get further than you could ever imagine in life.

Think back to a time when you had the opportunity to help another woman, whether it was giving her advice or just words of encouragement. What did you do with your opportunity? Did you take advantage of it and help uplift your sister, or did you choose not to?

Back when I was in college, the opportunity presented itself to lend a helping hand to a colleague who appeared to have been upset and crying. Now, I didn't know what happened or the reason behind her frustration, but I can remember her storming out and continuously saying things like, "Please just leave me alone, I don't want to talk right now." I was very quiet and would usually have never made such a big effort to see what was wrong, but I stepped out of my comfort zone despite the circumstances.

Sometimes the people who you think are the strongest and the people who are always there for others are the ones who need a shoulder to lean on the most. It is easy to portray a happy and positive image for others when that is all you know. Some women are accustomed to walking around each day with masks on that allow others to overlook their imperfections and only see perfect people who have it all together. Doing that takes an awful amount of strength as well as the ability to push through whatever may be going on within their lives.

However, when women start to empower each other, you will begin to see fewer women living day to day wearing invisible masks. You will notice more women effortlessly being comfortable with their imperfections and with their storms.

*To empower* means to make someone stronger and more confident—in themselves, in their lives, and in claiming their rights. It means to be able to pour your strength into another person and help them see the power that they possess. It means to enable and to be a giver. *Empower* means to uplift and to make others feel loved. It is something that some people do without noticing or thinking twice. It is also something that most people know how to do but choose not to do. It is a wonderful feeling that others receive when you empower them. American poet Maya Angelou once said, "I've learned that people will forget what you said, people will forget what you did, but people will never forget how you made them feel."

## Power of a Woman

There isn't one person living on earth who has never had a bad day or gone through something. But what most women fail to realize is how strong and powerful we all are. No matter their race, religion, size, or nationality, women possess so much power and strength mentally, physically, and emotionally. We are more powerful than the storms that are presented before us.

Look back at the times we were told we couldn't vote and had few, if any, rights. Now you see women voting, owning their own businesses, and even running for president. These things didn't just happen ironically or overnight. They happened because when women were told no, they kept going and didn't give up. Today, women still aren't offered equal pay for working the same exact job as men—you have some jobs and corporations where women may make eighty cents to every dollar men make. That isn't right, and society knows it isn't right.

Society as a whole has always empowered men, but what about women? Yes, men are supposed to lead, but who said women can't lead too? I'm not saying that women should be able to do everything that men do, because we weren't created to. That's what makes us so special. Many of the things that men lack or can't do, women can. That is where our power lies.

The power of a woman is impeccable. It is imperative that the new generation—and generations to come—understands this. Since society doesn't empower us, then it is mandatory that we empower each other. However, in today's generation, you see women looking down on other women, thinking that they are above them.

But in reality, it doesn't matter how much money you have, how pretty you are, your marital/relationship status, the type of car you drive, or the type of job you have. At the end of the day, we are all equal. Looking down on the next woman won't help you or her. However, lending a helping hand to the next woman will. Women should focus more on helping each other get ahead instead of trying to tear each other down and competing with one another. When you help others, it only puts you in a position to receive blessings. It's OK to have confidence and to be proud of your accomplishments, but when you look down on everyone else and think you are better than them, you will only hinder your success.

Oftentimes, women of all ages intentionally post degrading things about each other on social media—maybe because a woman's makeup isn't done right or her wardrobe is different from what you're familiar with. Well, guess what? Instead of gossiping about your sister, you could offer to show her how to do her makeup or suggest a better way to wear that outfit. There is always something you can do instead of degrading another woman for the things that she chooses to do or the way that she looks.

Some beauty is only skin deep, but knowing what it means to be *truly* beautiful is important. Real beauty is the way you carry yourself, how you treat others, and how you treat yourself. It's about the heart of a woman and having an unforgettable soul. You are beautiful in the skin you are in, and you don't need anyone to tell you. You have to know you are beautiful before anyone else can think you are. It doesn't matter if you are big, small, have long hair, or no hair. We are all beautiful in our own way.

It's OK to enhance yourself, whether you choose to work out every day to become fit, wear weave and makeup, or even decide to get surgery to fix your outer appearance. However, it becomes a problem when you then start to look at other women differently because they are not like you. That's when you should start looking within to assess the root of the problem—you. Everyone is different and that's what makes us all special and unique. No one has your smile, no one talks the way you do, and no one can ever be you. The world needs what you have. Imagine if everyone looked exactly the same and had the same personality, the same goals, the same talents, and the same demeanor. What do you think the world would be like? Would it make a difference if you were a part of the world? Probably not. But because you are different from everyone else, you add value to the world and to those around you. Therefore, don't be afraid to be yourself. Embrace every unique thing about yourself and you will realize how free you have become.

Many times, women will see a girl disrespecting and degrading herself and ruining her reputation and will laugh and talk about her. That makes them no better than the person they are looking down upon. Instead, they should pray for their sister, offer her advice, and try to help her. God made us all and no one is in a position to look down on anyone. What you think you have today can be taken away from you at any second, but a good heart and love for everyone will always stay with you. You have to learn to love your neighbor as yourself. The way you treat yourself and love yourself is a reflection of how you should treat those around you. Be willing to help other women make it to the top as well.

No one became successful on her own, not even you. It doesn't matter if it was your parents, a teacher, a friend, or a neighbor—someone paved the way, helped you, and taught you. Many times, we don't realize that our actions, as well as the actions of others (kindness, bitterness, jealousy, etc.), reflect the way we were raised. Your upbringing affects why you do most of the things the way that you do them.

Everyone was raised differently. That is an important fact to remember when you come across different types of people and wonder why they prioritize things a certain way or why they value certain things more than you do.

Some people were raised by older parents, while some were raised by younger parents. Some were raised by a single parent, and some people were not. So many factors play a part in making you the woman you become.

There are some women who were raped or molested as children. Some women grew up in poverty, some women grew up feeling unloved with a mind full of insecurities, and others may have experienced life with only one or neither of their parents in the home. As a child, you may have gone through unfortunate situations that you never had control over. But when you become an adult, it is up to you if you choose to let those situations define who you are or allow it to help you or possibly help another woman. Nothing that occurred in your past was a mistake—in order for you to be the woman you are at this very moment, you had to go through things that were probably a little uncomfortable to deal with. You may not like the ingredients for your future, but without them, you'll never know what the recipe is capable of making. In other words, if I was to tell you that you would be a billionaire tomorrow, then you would most likely be excited. But if I told you that it took being homeless—losing everything you have and not knowing where your next meal would come from—then you probably wouldn't like that. Your upbringing as a child may have been the same way. You may not have had the life you wanted or hoped for, but it was all necessary to create the person that you have become or will become.

The way you were raised is most likely a reflection of the way your parents were raised and the way you will raise your children. It is a cycle. For some women that is a good thing. For others, it could be unpleasant. Unless that cycle is broken, it will continue on throughout generations.

The power that women possess allows us to do so many things.

My mother would always tell me, "You are a woman that wears many hats." I would often wonder exactly what she meant by that. Eventually, I began to realize exactly what she was saying—that I, like other strong women, am able to handle the many tests that come my way and emerge like pure gold. Even though the tests may be hard, and even though I may have a lot on my plate, I wear many hats because I am the type of woman who gets those things done.

The number of things women do is striking. Whether it's cooking and cleaning, being a mother or wife, having a career, leading organizations, owning a business, volunteering, going to school, or whatever your calling may be, we as women are expected to do so much. And in doing all those things, sometimes we get tired. That's when the help and encouragement of our sisters comes in. Together we can accomplish so much more. We can make a difference. We can be the change that we want to see in the world.

## *The Storm*

> The thief comes only to steal
> and to kill and to destroy.
>
> —John 10:10

When we go through hardships, trials, and tribulations, it isn't always for us—it is because God will allow others going through the exact same thing to cross your path so they will have proof that they, too, will be able to get through the storm they are in. When storms arise, don't let them destroy you. Grow through whatever it is you are going through. Let it strengthen you. Let the storms you are faced with allow you to become better, not bitter. Like most storms, both literal and figurative, you don't always get to prepare for them.

They oftentimes happen unexpectedly and force you to face them head on. One of the hardest storms in my life occurred when everything was going great. I remember how happy I was and how much better my relationship with God had gotten. But one day changed it all. My grandmother passed away, and like all deaths, it's something you just have to deal with. After receiving the news, I packed my bags and got prepared to head out of state, to my grandmother's hometown. When I arrived, I attended the funeral and was ready to leave shortly after. However, my flight wasn't scheduled to depart for a couple of days, so I decided to spend a little time with my family. On the day of my departure, I said my good-byes to my family and was off to the airport. It was about five o'clock in the morning, and the sun was barely beginning to rise. On my way to catch my flight back home, something happened to my vehicle that caused me to lose control completely. To make matters worse, I was driving right beside an eighteen-wheeler truck when it happened. My vehicle veered back and forth between the eighteen-wheeler and a brick wall dividing the interstate before spinning around into oncoming traffic. After my vehicle stopped spinning, I sat there, dazed and incognizant. All I could see was blood everywhere, covering the airbags and the seats. Then headlights came my way, and I could hear horns being blown from vehicles that were about to hit me head on.

After the accident occurred, I was unable to eat and unable to talk. At that particular time, it took a huge toll on me and my life. Not being able to eat caused me to quickly lose weight and become very insecure. I was unhappy with the way I looked and discouraged because I was unable to do anything. I was about a month away from my twenty-first birthday, and not knowing how long the healing process would be, I only had one wish: to have the privilege of being able to eat again! I find it amazing how we take the little things in life for granted—things like walking, talking, eating, and being able to just do everything for yourself—until we are unable to do those things. I can remember being upset that God allowed something so terrible to happen. Because of the powerful impact, it took me a while to recover from the injuries mentally, physically, and emotionally, but the good thing is, time heals everything.

Through time, I was able to see that in the midst of the storm, God was the one covering me and keeping me safe. Although the scars and memories will forever be with me, I realize that God prevented a terrible situation from becoming a tragic one. Having women such as my mother, sister, and close friends remind me that everything would be OK is what gave me the strength to keep going. Now, when I see women going through similar things, being able to tell them that it all gets better with time brings me great joy, because I know deep down that it will.

Storms are nothing to play with. They are not fun and can even damage you if you allow them to. They come in different forms and most times, they come at you full force. For some women, the storm could be poverty (seeing everyone around you living freely and happily while you struggle with insufficient resources), homosexuality (not feeling accepted and feeling confused about life), abuse (experiencing emotional and physical pain), unforgiveness (struggling to find peace in your heart), sickness and disease (undergoing physical/mental attacks on your body or mind), and the list goes on and on.

The fact of the matter is, we all encounter storms. They won't always be easy to deal with, but know that God is always there. He'll be there to help you through every hard time you are faced with. You are not alone and never will be. When you walk into a storm with God, he will make sure you come out of it spotless, crystal clear, and beautiful, as though the storm never existed.

When a storm comes knocking on your door, be able to look adversity in the face with a confident mind-set, knowing you will overcome it. The devil comes to steal, kill, and destroy, and he will sneak in at the weakest and lowest points in your life. When you have a calling on your life and you are aware of it, the devil will come after you and try to destroy you in any and every way that he can. Have you ever noticed that when people are living any kind of way—living recklessly and in sin—the devil doesn't bother them? But when they begin to follow God's way of living, problems they have never encountered start to occur, and attacks come left and right? That is because Satan didn't see them as a threat before. There was no need to try to take them out or harm them, because they were satisfying him by not following God and his divine way of living. When you follow God, you can expect attacks from Satan, but you never have to worry about him winning. Remember,

> *Blessed is the one who perseveres under trial because, having stood the test, that person will receive the crown of life that the Lord has promised to those who love him.*
>
> —James 1:12

Therefore, keep God first and remain the strong confident woman you are. Never be ashamed to talk about what made you into the woman you have become, because you may never know it, but your story could save another woman's life. And that's what it is all about: we all have to go through this journey of life, so why not try to make it as easy as possible for others? Help your sister up when she is down, because the time will come when you will need a helping hand. Two is always better than one. When two of us face a storm, we are much more likely to defeat it—as opposed to it defeating us.

Know that even though you may be experiencing tough times, things could be a lot worse. Learn to appreciate the little things that are going right instead of focusing on the negatives. Choose to see the positive aspects of every situation before you begin to complain or feel sorry for yourself. And believe me, no matter what your situation may be or how bad things may look, there is always something positive within the storms you encounter. I have seen women lose everything they had due to unfortunate situations, such as house fires and strong tropical hurricanes. But the beauty in it is that they were still thankful: They appreciated the fact that they were alive and in their right minds. They knew that material things could always be replaced. Most times, the good outweighs the bad.

## Knowing Who You Are

> Do not conform to the pattern of this world, but
> be transformed by the renewing of your mind.
> —Romans 12:2

Growing up with both of my parents allowed me to learn a lot. I was able to learn how to be a woman, and I was shown how a man was supposed to treat me. I can remember how every time I got in the car with my father, he would open my car door for me. As I got older, of course, so did my father. I would periodically go home for breaks in college, and I can remember my father walking around to open my car door—even while walking with a cane. I remember thinking how amazing that moment was for me and how I have always had an example of what a man is supposed to be like.

I am aware that there are many women who have never had the privilege of being taught about self-worth or how they are supposed to be treated by men. Therefore, when I come across women, whether they are my friends, acquaintances, or complete strangers, I talk to them about self-worth and how important it is to love yourself. Whether they take my advice or not, I have done my part. That's what many women should understand: you can't make anyone listen or take heed to what you are saying, but if you don't reach out when you see fit, then what choice would they have?

Many times, men look at how women treat each other and think that it is OK to treat us the same way. If women refrain from bashing other women and disrespecting each other, then perhaps men will begin to do the same. It has to start somewhere, and women hold the power to initiate that change.

If you see a woman who is happily married or in a committed relationship, then leave her and her partner alone. I've seen too many women knowingly interfere in other women's relationships. Ladies, we are better than that. There is someone for everyone. If a man is aware that you possess little to no morals, then he will treat you as such. Respect yourself, and learn to respect your sister. A little respect will take you a long way, and when you have respect for yourself, it shows in everything you do.

Self-respect is something to value. You must first love yourself in order to have self-respect. Loving yourself is a choice. When you choose to love yourself, you are choosing to take care of *you* before all else. Take care of your mental, physical, and spiritual health, as well as your emotional well-being. If you are not taken care of first, then how can you expect to be in a position to help others? You must gather strength yourself before trying to pour it into anyone else; otherwise, you'll be left empty.

Knowing yourself means knowing your worth. Some of the choices you make in life are based on your self-worth—the way you view yourself and how much you value yourself. You should understand that self-esteem and self-worth are traits that numerous women struggle with each day, and that is OK. Know that without a doubt, you are special and greatly significant to this world. You should love yourself and embrace who you are. Loving yourself is loving the way you walk, the way you talk, the hair that grows on your head, and every little freckle upon your body.

Loving yourself is choosing to be yourself in a world that tries to change you into someone you are not meant to be. That is what you call *strength*. It takes a strong woman to stay true to herself, and it all starts in the mind. When you truly love yourself, you don't settle for mediocracy—not in your career, not in relationships, and not with your dreams. Why settle when the only limits are the ones you have stipulated in your mind?

You can do absolutely anything if you adjust your mind to it. If you don't love yourself, then how can you expect someone else to? You must set the bar for the way you desire to be treated by others. When you are real with yourself, then you can be real with others as well. Being real with yourself means telling yourself exactly the way you see things, not just the way you want things to be. Only when you acknowledge the way things are can you work towards fixing them.

Never let anyone tell you who you are; you must know that for yourself. Knowing who you are is key to getting where you want to be in life. Sometimes, you may need to lose yourself in order to find yourself. Finding yourself is an essential part of life, no matter how long it may take. Even if you have to do some soul-searching, by all means, find out who you really are. In doing so, you become one with yourself and, in most cases, that will bring you the peace and love you desire.

When you find yourself, you find out what you really like, what you don't like, what you stand for, and what's important to you. You don't make drastic decisions against your will, and you begin to become transparent. It is OK to be your natural self—it will attract people of your kind. Some areas in your life will start to become a little less perplexing as you find out who you really are.

# Accountability Partners

> Brothers, if someone is caught in a sin, you who are spiritual should restore him gently. But watch yourself, or you also may be tempted. Carry each other's burdens, and in this way you will fulfill the law of Christ.
>
> —Galatians 6:1–2

Connecting with people who know the real you will allow you to find an accountability partner. Every woman needs an accountability partner. It's someone who knows you well enough to help you stay on track, to hold you accountable for your actions—a person you can depend on to give you the best advice specifically for you. She may help with goals you set, dreams you said you'd go after, a religious journey you are on, or any unique personal asset within your life. An accountability partner will make sure you stay on the right path for whatever it is you are working toward in life. When you are at your lowest points in life, aside from God, your accountability partner is the person you should be able to depend on to uplift you and get you back to being the person he or she knows you to be. Find an accountability partner who can help you analyze your situations, who knows when to respond and when to just let things be as they are—someone who knows that not everything needs a reaction.

But you need a *good* accountability partner. Back in college, when I was going through a breakup, I needed advice, and the one person I decided to go to told me to retaliate: post defaming things on social media in hopes of ruining things for the person who I'd been in a relationship with. Now, although I'd been completely disrespected in this relationship, retaliating in a negative way is something I was strictly against and would have never done regardless of the situation. It went against what I believed in and who I was as a person. It interfered with my character and individual morals. But by listening to and taking bad advice from someone I saw as an accountability partner, my peace of mind was destroyed. It took a while for me to get over the fact that I'd done something completely against what I stood for.

That is why it is so important to have an accountability partner who knows the real you and what you stand for as an individual. This will be a great asset in your future. Realize that even though you may have an accountability partner, you will still make mistakes. That is what life is about. Grow and live life; don't just go through the motions. If you don't make mistakes as a woman, then you aren't growing. Mistakes are made for you to learn from them. Never hold anyone to their past mistakes, because no one is perfect. Be aware of your perception of perfection. If we made ourselves, then of course everyone would be perfect, because we would have the opportunity to choose the ideal life for ourselves. As long as you don't make the same mistake repeatedly, then you are fine. But if you do, then that is proof that you are not learning from it.

As women, we sometimes hold ourselves to past mistakes, which is not a healthy decision. You must learn and move on or your life will become stagnant, with lots of regrets. Be aware of what is causing you to fail in different areas of your life and what mistakes you may be making. They don't define who you are. Don't feel condemned by your past mistakes, because every day is a new day to become a better you. It is a new opportunity at life.

It doesn't matter what you have been through, what storms you had to face, and what sins you may have committed; God can still use you. If you had a child out of wedlock, guess what? God can still use you. If you have a record of lying or being deceitful, guess what? God can use you as well. He can still birth something wonderful and magnificent out of you. Your talents and gifts won't be taken away from you or go to waste because of mistakes you may have made in the past. God can turn your past into a beautiful miracle if you let him. Use your accountability partner to help you rise up, and stop putting yourself down. When you repent, God forgives you. You must then forgive yourself and make a conscious decision to do better. Your problems and your storms are not bigger than God. Put it all in God's hands and leave it there. Let him use you instead of letting yourself be used by people. Let him show you that despite everything you have been through in life, you are still worthy of the blessings he has for you.

Mistakes, as well as failure, are only a setup for success. Think about what success looks like to you. How do you define success? Is it something materialistic, or is it something that can't be bought? Success doesn't look the same for everyone. Some may think that success is winning the lottery. Others may think that success is owning a house. Depending on where you are in life and what you value most, your perception of success will differ. However, without experiencing failure, you'll never know what success feels like. Don't let failure discourage you; allow it to motivate you. Keep trying in whatever it is that you are trying to succeed in. If failure is a part of the storm you are in, then appreciate it, because after the storm, you'll be able to enjoy the perk of having gone through it—success.

You'll get there. Don't be afraid to fail. Success doesn't come with an easy roadmap. It takes sacrifice and dedication. It requires you to go through some detours and roadblocks. Sure, everyone wants success, but few are willing to work hard enough for it. Success doesn't just come to you; you have to go and get it. When you are working toward attaining prosperity, depending on what your goal is, you have to be strong enough to take a couple of no's until people have no choice but to say yes. Be willing to fail as many times as it takes you to get to the finish line and win. Don't let failure turn you into a quitter. Never give up no matter what.

If you find yourself failing in too many areas of your life, know that it's OK to make a couple of changes to adjust. Change is often a good thing, and sometimes, it is necessary. If you do decide to change, make sure it's for the better. Don't do it because someone told you to or to please anyone except for yourself. And don't change to keep someone in your life: not your so-called friends and especially not a man. If the people in your life accept you completely, then they won't demand change.

You have to want to change for yourself. When you really want it, it will show. Don't just talk about change; work on yourself. You will come to find that when you work on yourself, the result becomes one of your biggest assets.

\*

> Kind words are like honey—sweet to the soul and healthy for the body.
>
> —Proverbs 16:24

When storms show up, know that it is OK to talk about your problems. Communication is key. You will see that it will help you mentally and emotionally. But first, women must learn to talk to each other peacefully and respectfully without judging each other. That's when you will see a huge difference in the world around you. Women must be understanding during times of triumph and listen more than they speak.

Communication is a vital part of life; a lack of it will damage any relationship. When you communicate effectively and respectfully, it puts you in a totally different league. It is absurd that some women will have a problem with you if you just look their way. But it is because they lack the ability to communicate with other women adequately. Never let that change you from the woman you are. Don't allow people or society to dictate or control your inner being. If you see a woman and she doesn't greet you or speak to you, that is OK. Speak to her anyway. When women learn that it is OK to be kind to other women, that's when things become magical. Learn to be kind, but never let anyone take advantage of your kindness.

Letting your guard down enough to communicate effectively with other women is essential. This isn't to say that you must be friends with everyone you come across but that you should be kind enough to speak, give a compliment, or hold a conversation when needed. Realize that everyone has a bad day sometimes. If you are offended by the way someone may have said something, consider the fact that maybe she isn't having a good day before you hold that against her or start an argument.

Oftentimes, I see women in businesses and stores attempting to get another woman fired from her job because the worker didn't say hello, appeared to be upset, or had an attitude. But to those women, I would suggest this: Think about one of the worst days of your life and how you felt during that time. That may have been exactly how the woman working was feeling when she didn't greet you as you walked through the door. So instead of calling her place of business to get her fired, tell her that everything will be OK or do something that will make her day a little easier. Let others see the good in you before automatically showing them the evil in you. Always be kind, because you never know what someone is going through.

Consider the fact that everyone goes through storms at some point in their lives. If it is your friend, family member, or anyone close to you, don't end the relationship on bad terms. That is never a good idea. Be able to communicate. Be able to consider reconciliation with those who may have hurt you or stoned you. Never let the sun set while you're still mad at someone, because you never know when their sun is scheduled to set. Life is too short for you to hold grudges.

# Role Models

> When I was a child, I talked like a child,
> I thought like a child, I reasoned like
> a child. When I became a man, I put
> the ways of childhood behind me.
>
> —1 Corinthians 13:11

Having positive women in the spotlight—such as actors, singers, and models—for young girls to look up to is important. Everywhere you look, you see our youths with either phones in their hands, their eyes glued to the television, or their ears hooked to the radio. Whether you realize it or not, these young girls are learning.

They are learning from the rap songs that talks about money, sex, and drugs. They are learning from the reality shows they watch on television. And they are learning about superficial looks from women in magazines. They are seeing in advertisements and billboards how women are treated as sexual objects and symbols instead of as the bold bright women they actually are.

Teaching our girls about following their dreams and how important education is could impact the world so much more. In order to see a difference in generations to come, our little girls must be taught something different than what the media are showing them. They need real guidance, especially growing up in today's society.

If they are not taught at a young age about etiquette and how to be ladies, then what do you expect them to be like when they become adults? Knowing how to carry themselves and how to transition from little girls into young women is essential. Teach them to not expose themselves and to cherish their bodies. They should learn at an early age how they should be treated, whether a man is in the home or not.

For example, having different men in and out of the house. If you have multiple men repeatedly entering into your home, then your little girl will think that is normal and that she should have the same experience when she gets older. Another example is abusing drugs and other substances. If you don't want your child growing up to do the things that he or she sees you doing, then why let them see you doing it? It all starts with the parent, who must lead by example. Take responsibility for the things you expose your children to. Take heed of the Bible verse in Proverbs 22:6 where it says, "Train up a child in the way he should go: and when he is old, he will not depart from it." Parents must be leaders in showing their children what is acceptable and what isn't. Little girls should be taught that life isn't fair and everything won't always go their way. Teach them what to do when they experience injustice and how to react when it occurs.

Maybe you're not a parent—but that doesn't mean you are exempt from positively impacting our little girls. Children can't teach themselves. They are learning from someone, and that someone is you. You have kids all around you, whether they are your nieces, cousins, or children at church or in your neighborhood. They are watching you. They pay attention even when you think they are not.

Little girls should be taught about morals and respect. In today's society, morals have been pushed to the side. The world has devalued what's most important. Therefore it is our duty to teach children what is important. They should be taught how to respect one another and how to respect themselves. How to say "yes, ma'am" and "yes, sir," and to use "Mrs." or "Ms." and "Mr." Nowadays, you have older people saying they don't like to be called "Ms." or "ma'am." They may say things like, "Oh, that makes me sound old." But what they fail to realize is that when children say those things, they are showing a sign of respect. By telling them not to call you "Mr." or "Mrs." and not to say "yes, ma'am" and "no, sir," you are telling them that they don't have to respect you.

I grew up in a home where if I just said "yes" to my mother or father, they would repeat the words "yes, *ma'am*" or "yes, *sir*" until I said it. My parents taught me the importance of respecting my grandparents and anyone older than me. They showed me that I could learn a plethora of things from old and wise adults like my grandparents. And they were right.

No matter their level of authority, children should always respect those around them. Little girls must know that they should treat a janitor with the same respect as they would treat the president. They will come to find out that respect will take them very far. Teaching them not to be followers will build up a generation of leaders. We need strong leaders in this world, and teaching them while they are young is key.

Learn to be a positive mentor and role model to young girls. They need it now more than ever. Show them that there is more to life than short skirts, boys, and makeup. They need to know that it is OK to be themselves and have fun but also know when to put fun aside and be about business when it is time. They should be taught while they are young about where they come from and the importance of family.

There is so much hate in this world, and it usually begins at an early age. Children don't just grow up hating one another. They learn from their upbringing and the people around them. Teach our little girls to not see race, color, or religion but to see a person's heart instead. Teach them how to love and be loved.

One will not see a difference unless these actions persist. Women empowerment means empowering *all* women regardless of age, nationality, social status, health, or intellectual abilities. No one should be excluded. We all need each other. This includes friends, family, strangers, and even our enemies:

> *But love your enemies do good to them, and lend to them without expecting to get anything back.*
> —Luke 6:35

Even though you may not get anything from helping our little girls or teaching them right from wrong, know that it makes a statement when you decide to help others even when it doesn't benefit you, such as those who can never repay you. When you don't look for anything in return and act purely out of the generosity of your heart, it speaks volumes.

Every Sunday, I would get up bright and early to attend church service. I always went by myself, because I was hours away from my family and I didn't have any peers or friends who liked to attend church the way I did. On one particular Sunday, a friend of mine asked to attend church with me. I was excited, and of course, I said yes. As we get to church, service was going great, and the word was amazing. As we approached the end of service and the pastor gave the invitation to join, I can remember my friend looking at me with tears in her eyes, asking if I would walk with her. I was ecstatic.

Now, to remind you, I was already a member. I'd taken that long walk down to the altar by myself already. I didn't want to do it again. Just the thought of having to get up in front of a huge congregation while everyone looked and stared made me a bit nervous. At that time, two things were going through my mind: that "if you deny your father on earth, then he will deny you in heaven," and the fact that this was bigger than me—it was about someone who wanted to have a relationship with God, and the only thing stopping her was the fear of doing it alone.

So I got up and walked with her. After all, she was my friend, and I wanted the best for her. By walking down to the altar with my fellow sister, I didn't get anything, but she did. Sometimes, you have to put your selfish ways aside to help someone else.

Realize that it isn't always about you. Know that life isn't a marathon. Everyone can make it to the finish line if we help one another. If you see another woman struggling to make it through the journey of life, it's OK to stop and help her up so you both can make it together. It gets lonely at the top, so why not have someone up there with you? Don't try to live in this world alone; it wasn't made for that.

Many women begin to isolate themselves from the world for various reasons. It could be because of a bad breakup or divorce, low self-esteem, or the loss of a loved one. But no one should go through any of these things alone, and these are not valid reasons for you to isolate yourself. Isolation can be helpful when you want to change or better yourself and you need time away from the world to do so. Use isolation for a beneficial purpose as opposed to an unhealthy one; that kind of isolation can sometimes lead to depression, which is never a good thing. It affects your well-being and takes a toll on you and your life. It makes you feel bound and trapped. Alone and empty. As you may know, depression can even lead to suicide.

There is absolutely no reason that you—or any woman—should feel the need to end your life because you can't deal with your problems alone. There is always another woman willing to help you through the tough times you encounter. If you are faced with a storm that results in depression, that is OK. Most women experience depression at some point in their lives. Learning to pick yourself back up from being down and depressed is key. Never let hard times keep you down; we are all human, and we all experience them.

When the storms in your life hit, be able to stand tall and tell yourself, you are more than a conqueror. You will, without a doubt, see victory. There is life and death in the power of your tongue. Therefore, you should speak positivity over your life. Yes, women should encourage other women, but sometimes you have to encourage yourself too. You have to speak life into yourself. No one can love you the way you love yourself. It all starts with the person in the mirror. You won't always be able to rely on your friends or your parents or a significant other to be there for you and motivate you. Learn to motivate yourself and have confidence in everything you do and everything you say. Have confidence in your dreams and have confidence in your future. Confidence will take you far.

Having confidence does not mean you should have a presumptuous or boastful attitude. It means you should acknowledge your capabilities and qualities, but you should still be able to give credit to others where it is due. When you see another woman excel in something, receive a promotion at work, or achieve a lifelong dream, be able to congratulate her and be happy for her. No, don't *pretend* to be happy for her—you have to genuinely be happy for her.

If you are wondering why other women are succeeding more than you or receiving all the blessings you may have prayed and hoped for, consider that perhaps it isn't your season yet. Everything and everyone has a season. Whether it is a season of prosperity or a season of failure, a season of financial stability or a season of struggle, or perhaps a season of waiting. Seasons come and seasons go. Some seasons may last longer than others. While going through your different seasons, appreciate the beauty in them. You won't like every season, but every season is crucial to get you to where you are meant to be in life.

Don't complain when the storms appear. If you can take the good and be happy, then why complain about the bad? In life you must accept both the good and the bad. The different seasons will either make you or break you. Be strong enough to withstand the many seasons and storms that come your way. They won't last forever. All storms are temporary.

When you encounter a storm in life, know that something great is about to occur. God doesn't send us through storms just because he wants to torture or hurt us. He allows us to go through storms for a divine purpose: to birth something out of us, to make us stronger for the next stages of our lives, and to help us develop into the women we are meant to be. Sometimes, God uses storms to get our attention. Maybe you've been doing things your own way for far too long, and God needs you to open your eyes to his ways. Maybe you know the word of God and right from wrong but have chosen to put your righteous ways aside to live the way of the world, trying to please man as opposed to pleasing God. No matter what the case may be, storms are brought upon us for a specific purpose. Pay close attention to what that purpose might be.

Despite the uncomfortable tests and trials you experience in life, know that every storm ends with victory. After the storm, you'll be stronger and even more beautiful than you were going in. Think about James 1:2–4, the Bible verse where it says, "Consider it pure joy, my brothers and sisters, whenever you face trials of any kinds, because you know that the testing of your faith produces perseverance. Let perseverance finish its work so that you may be mature and complete, not lacking anything." You should be proud of yourself because you held on long enough to make it through a tough season. When these tough seasons finally blow over, you must remember where God brought you from and where he has taken you.

You should remain humble even in times when you are not going through anything. Why? Because when you are not going through a storm, someone else is. Be able to remain humble enough to reach back and help someone else who is going through a tough season in life.

These seasons can also be called "chapters" within your life. When one chapter closes, you have to move on so you can get to the next chapter. There are some women who try to stay in one chapter too long and others who try to jump into a new chapter before it is time. Know when to close a chapter and when to wait until the chapter is complete. Be patient. A season takes time and must run its course. Don't be so eager to step into something you aren't equipped and ready for. Your current season is meant to get you ready for what is to come, and stepping into things prematurely can interfere with your next season. Be willing to wait.

Patience can be the difference between receiving something of excellent value and being given something that is mediocre. Having the patience to wait for something is a respectable character trait that requires discipline and self-control. Don't become weary or give up on what you are waiting for. Be willing to accept the delay, and be able to endure and persevere. In due season, you will reap the benefits of having been patient. Patience is a virtue, and patience is key.

> The vision is for a future time. It describes the
> end, and it will be fulfilled. If it seems slow in
> coming, wait patiently, for it will surely take place.
> It will not be delayed.
>
> —Habakkuk 2:3

# *What Is Your Chapter Called?*

Every chapter in your life has a title.
Right now, my chapter is called "Patiently Awaiting."

What chapter are you on in life? _____

_____.

Timing is everything. Don't try to keep up with anyone, because many of the people you try to keep up with won't have the same purpose in life as you. Different callings and different purposes require going through different stages at different times. Move at your own pace and speed, but make sure it is in the right direction. Be willing to ask God to guide you and to direct your path so you can walk into your destiny.

When you find your purpose, you will find life to be much more meaningful. Your purpose is what sets you apart from everyone else in the world. When you are living out your purpose, you must be willing to put the standards of society to rest. Be willing to stand out and live as the person you are meant to be, doing what you are meant to do. Forget what everyone else around you is doing. When you start focusing on what everyone else is doing, then you begin to lose track of what you should be doing and where you should be headed. Focus on you. Sometimes you may need to use tunnel vision and block out where everyone else is in life, pinpoint where you want to be, and have an action plan on how to get there. Your purpose is for you and you only. It is specially selected for you by God himself. You have absolutely everything you need—such as skills, resources, and knowledge—to live out your purpose. It is what you were created for and put here on earth to accomplish. No one can take that away.

Be aware that everyone has special skills and talents. What we do with them is up to us. If you have a skill, and you see another woman struggling to do something you can practically do with your eyes closed, offer to help her. What may be easy for one woman might be difficult for you, and that is OK. Find out what you have to offer the world and what you are good at—not just what your parents want you to be good at or what will make you a lot of money. Sure, everyone wants a job or career that makes good money, but know that there is something out there you are passionate about that could also benefit you financially. You just have to think and be willing to use your God-given skills and talents.

If I could become a singer or even a basketball player, perhaps I would. However, I am aware that I wasn't born with a beautiful singing voice like Beyoncé, and I don't think a five-foot woman would be the best on the court. But I do possess other talents that God saw fit for me to have and work with. And that is the mentality you need when considering what is for you and what isn't.

It is OK if you don't have life all figured out. You're not supposed to. Life is a journey, and only a perfect person is capable of having life completely figured out—and we all know that no one is perfect. Therefore, you have to work for what you want; especially us women. Encourage other women to be all that they can be. Go after everything that society told you that you couldn't have. Take control of your future. You have the power to write your own story. No one can create your future except you. Go out and dominate. Be fierce and don't settle for "no." You'll be glad you didn't.

If there is something you are truly passionate about, then go after it. Many times, the things that interest you the most and the things that you feel strongest about are connected to your calling and purpose in life. Pay close attention to the little details of where your interests navigate. Be willing to work like you've never worked before. Put your all into it, and make your dreams your reality.

If your dreams and goals look and sound impossible to achieve, that's most likely a good thing. It means you aren't selling yourself short or settling for something mediocre. If what you are trying to achieve has a short, direct, and simple road map, then perhaps you should challenge yourself to dream bigger.

Achieving big goals and dreams and walking into your calling won't be easy. It may require experiencing a few storms to get you prepared for what you are going to receive—to get you to your end goal. And many times, when you have dreams and goals that you can see, you can't always show them to everyone. They won't be able to see the visions that God has given you. But your purpose is found in God, not people. Depending on what you are going after in life, some people will laugh at you and tell you that you can't do it. They may even call you crazy for thinking you can achieve something so big. This is the reason you can't tell everyone your dreams: They will kill them. They will discourage you, and before you know it, that dream you once had, that vision you once saw so clearly, or that goal you had set, won't be there anymore. Because other people are afraid to go after their own dreams, they will try to talk you into thinking you aren't capable of achieving yours either. Small people have small minds.

That is why you should surround yourself with women who have the same goals as you. Connect with other women with like mind-sets. If you aspire to be a billionaire one day, then pay attention to a billionaire's mind-set. If you want to start your own business, get a doctorate degree, or buy a new car, then surround yourself with those who are on the same path as you or those who have already done it. That will help you tremendously. The same advice applies if you want to be married one day. You can't dream and pray for a husband but hang out with women who don't believe in relationships or marriage. They will soon persuade you into thinking the way they do. Have a strong mind and connect with those who are on the same level as you mentally.

Also, be aware of your energy. If you want happiness, then be happy. Never allow anyone to steal your joy, because the Lord giveth and the Lord taketh—mankind does not have the power to do that. If you want peace, then have a peaceful spirit. What you put out is often what you will receive. Energy is transferable. Have positive energy and connect with other women who acquire the same energy as you. If you are a happy person who is always in a good mood, and all of a sudden, you start to spend time with a person who has an abominably sad attitude, then that negative energy will start to erode your positivity. Be careful whom you spend most of your time with, because those people are oftentimes a reflection of you. Yes, you should help those individuals when you see fit, but it doesn't mean you have to wrap your life around their lives. Protect your peace. Not everyone needs access to you and what you have to offer. Feed your spirit and your thoughts positivity and you will see those vibes flourish within you.

Along with dreaming big and accompanying women on the same mission as yourself, make time for prayer. Prayer will help you fulfill your dreams and goals and identify your calling. It will help you get through some of the toughest storms in life. I know this may be something you have heard a thousand times, but prayer actually changes things. When you pray, it makes a difference.

Prayer has been the biggest asset in my entire life, and I learned its importance at a young age. Growing up, my parents would always take my three older siblings and me to church. I remember participating in all the church plays and singing in the choir, even when I didn't want to. But when I got a little older (maybe age twelve or thirteen), I decided to give my life to Christ and profess Jesus as my Lord and Savior. Nothing changed immediately except the fact that I knew if I prayed and called on God, he would be there. I knew I'd never have to worry or want for anything, because God would provide. I knew that prayer was just as important as taking that first step toward having a relationship with God.

Over the years, as I became an adult, I realized that just because you pray for something, it doesn't mean you will automatically receive it. God may have better plans for you, or he may be protecting you from something you thought you wanted. You also have to come to terms with the fact that God doesn't always answer you at your convenience or when you want him to. That doesn't mean you should stop praying; it means you should continue to pray until you receive an answer to your prayer. Pray *harder*.

It doesn't matter if it is sickness you need healing from or a test you can't seem to pass. Pray. Learn to pray about your situations before taking your problems to anyone else. No one can help you the way God can. There is power in prayer. Those times when you're at your lowest, when you feel like no one is there, pray. When you feel lost and in need of guidance through life, pray. No matter what storm, test, or trial comes at you, pray your way through it.

Prayer has helped me get through every storm I have ever encountered. It helped me get through many of the lonely times life has hit me with. Not only did prayer help me get to college, but it got me through college as well. It helped me during times when I thought I'd lose my mind. Even those times when I felt like quitting and giving up. With prayer, I persevered.

If you are not accustomed to praying, then it won't hurt to give it a try. You can even write your prayer down just so you have a reference to go back to and look at when your prayer is answered. You will begin to acknowledge that prayer is a huge asset to your life as well. When you pray, don't just pray for little things. Pray for big things that you know you could never accomplish on your own. That's when you'll know that prayer has served a purpose in your life. Learn to pray and leave everything you prayed for in God's hands. It makes absolutely no sense to pray to God and then continue worrying or attempting to fix your problems yourself:

> Do not be anxious about anything but in everything by prayer and supplication with thanksgiving let your requests be made known to God, which surpasses all understanding, will guard your hearts and your minds in Christ Jesus.
> —Philippians 4:6–7

When you pray, you also have to work for what you are praying for. You can't just pray, asking God to help you with something, and then wait, thinking that it will magically appear at your front door. If it is a new job you are praying for, then perhaps you should be putting in applications every chance you get. If it is new friendships you hope to attain, then get out of your house so you can meet new people. If it is an addiction you need help with, then stop hanging around people who influence you to continue. Whatever your case may be, you can't pray but then live a life opposite of what you are praying for. You'll never see your prayers answered. Put yourself in a position to receive blessings. Prepare for them.

If the Lord has said that something is for you, then nothing and no one in heaven, hell, or on earth can stop it. You don't have to compete. You will receive everything that is meant for you.

Most of all, have faith in what you pray for. If you are praying to get through a tough storm, have faith that you will. Faith is believing in the unknown despite the current circumstances. No matter what your situation may look like or how bad your storm may be, if you believe and have faith that everything will be all right, then it will be. Having faith and having a relationship with God will take you a long way.

Having a relationship with God is more than just dressing up on Sunday mornings for church and having a few Bible verses memorized. Christ should live in you. No matter where you are, your actions should reveal the relationship you have with God. When people see you, they should automatically know that you are connected with God. They should be able to tell you apart from the nonbelievers, and you should stand out in a room full of people. Everyone that you come in contact with should be able to see God's heart through your actions. You can't just read the word; you must also be a *doer* of the word. Having an intimate relationship with God, where you feel comfortable just talking to him and giving him all your worries and problems, can make a huge difference.

Many of the storms you will go through and difficult occurrences happening in the world today are in the Bible. When you study the Bible and do as the Bible says, you'll see that every problem has a solution.

Trust God. It is he who will get you through the storms of life. Not your followers on social media, not those men or women who you've been trying to impress, and not your friends. If you make sure your relationship with God is right, then he will make sure everything else is taken care of. When you learn to fully submit yourself to God and repent, then you will see areas in your life change for the better. Will life be perfect? Of course not. Will you still experience storms and problems? Yes, you will. But will you have to worry about those storms defeating you, and will you have to live life wondering and worrying about what tomorrow will bring? No. God will have you covered. He knows your today, your tomorrow, and your future.

Fully surrendering yourself to God means being able to trust him with your whole life—not just certain areas of your life. It means you trust that he knows what you need and has your best interests at heart. God knows what you need before you even think you need it. He knows when to give you the blessings that your heart desires. Sometimes God wants to mature you so that you can handle the blessings that he wants to give you. Don't worry, God knows what he is doing and can see things you can't. When you fully trust God, you'll begin to feel a sense of peace. When you have peace in your life, mind, and spirit, everything around you can be shattering into pieces, but because God has showered you with peace, nothing will be able to disturb or bother you. You'll be able to get sleep at night instead of worrying yourself to death about something you can't control. Be able to cast all your worries upon God and let him take care of everything that is or has been bothering you. He can handle it a lot better than you can.

# Empowering Women with Love

> Love is patient love is kind. It does not
> envy it does not boast, it is not proud.
> —1 Corinthians 13:4

When choosing to empower women through the storms they are facing, you must do so with love.

Love is the key to life. Without it, imagine what the world would be like. I imagine that it would be a world full of hate and bitterness. Love will overpower hate. The sad reality is that the world we live in is literally at war. There is not enough love produced in the world around us. Every time you turn on the television, what do you see? War! We are at war like never before. We are hurting and killing one another, and for what? Because we were mad at the moment? Or because our pride was hurt? Whatever the reason may be, it is not worth hurting another individual or taking another person's life. And I say "we" because we *are* our brothers and sisters. When you take a look around, you see people fighting, robbing, and killing one another. I've even seen women set other women up to be raped, beaten, and tortured by those they called friends. This isn't love. And these hateful, constant, reoccurring acts happen far too often.

You may be thinking, "Well, I don't do any of those things, so I'm not at war with anyone." Wrong. If you are living in this world, then you are at war. Which side you are on is the question. Are you adding to the problem or taking away from the problem? Are you promoting empowerment or exploitation? Are you choosing to lend a helping hand? Or watching your sister suffer alone? Are you producing love or hate?

Learn to love your sister with a genuine heart. It'll make all the difference in the world. When you are genuine, love is automatically present. It is the root of happiness. If you want to be happy, then show love to others. You will see that it will be reciprocated in one way or another. When you put out love, you will receive it in turn. It may not always be from the same person you poured love into, but if you pay attention, you'll see that love comes right back to you.

There are so many ways to show love and the goodness within your heart. It can be something as simple as letting someone else get the parking spot you were waiting on, offering to let someone in front of you while waiting in line at the grocery store, or volunteering to help another individual, or just doing something for someone when it doesn't benefit you. You can show love with kind gestures, such as giving a compliment, smiling, or doing whatever you think will brighten someone else's day. It can be expressing gratitude and showing that you appreciate others. There are so many things that can be done daily to show love. Choosing to show love to others demonstrates a lot about your character and who you are as a person. Learn to love your neighbor just as much as you love yourself. That's what we as humans were created for: to help one another and to do so with love.

Being able to love others the way you love yourself requires you to do just that: love *yourself*. When you see others treating people poorly, robbing or abusing them, it is because they don't love themselves. If they deeply loved themselves, it would show in their treatment of others.

There have been many times when I have passed by homeless individuals who were standing in the street, holding a sign. Now, I may not have had any money to give to them, but you don't always have to have money to be a blessing. I looked around to see what I had that would benefit them in some way, whether it was a bottle of water, lunch that I'd just bought for myself, or a blanket. I used what I had to be a blessing to someone else, even if it meant giving up something that I wanted. Showing love requires you to be selfless—to be able to put others before yourself.

Many times, we get so caught up in the world and with society that we end up losing ourselves trying to keep up. We forget to love ourselves and love our sisters. Stop. Take a deep breath, look in the mirror, and refocus on what's important. Know that love is a choice, not a feeling. You don't just give love to others because you feel like it. You may experience many days where you don't feel like being kind or helping someone else or whatever the case may be. Does that mean you should stop showing love to others? No. It means you should put your feelings to the side and make a conscious decision to choose love.

Be able to love those who envy you and show love to those who have wronged you. You may be thinking, "Why should I love someone who doesn't love me or has hurt me?" Well, God still loved you even at times when you made mistakes and put him last. Consider 1 John 3:16–18, where it says, "This is how we know what love is: Jesus Christ laid down his life for us. And we ought to lay down our lives for our brothers and sisters. If anyone has material possessions and sees a brother or sister in need but has no pity on them, how can the love of God be in that person? Dear children, let us not love with words or speech but with actions and in truth."

I'm sure everyone has encountered at least one person who may have said "I love you" but never showed it. Sure, anyone can easily say the words *I love you*, but love is an action. You must show others that you love them, not just verbally express it as though that is enough.

You may also be thinking, "Loving my enemy and loving everyone just as I love myself isn't easy." Of course it isn't. If it was easy, everyone would be doing it. Most of the things in life that aren't the easiest are the things that are most valuable and will get you the furthest in life.

Love is an important principle to keep in mind all the days of your life. If you find someone talking down to you or treating you poorly, retaliate with love. You will see that doing so will either upset or shock her, because she didn't expect such a kind reaction after behaving so unjustly, and she'll begin to regret treating you that way. She'll apologize or just leave you alone altogether because she didn't get the hostile reaction she was expecting.

Never be afraid to love: "There is no fear in love, but perfect love casts out fear. For fear has to do with punishment, and whoever fears has not been perfected in love" (1 John 4:18). Loving others is the one thing you can do that is free. It requires no expense and hardly any effort. To say that loving others is always easy would be delusive. However, loving others will take you far in life and will empower those whom you pour love into. Love will cast out evil, and it will cast out hate. Love can conquer all.

## Key Points to Take Away

To get through a tough storm, you'll need to know who you are and how to use your power as a woman; have an accountability partner, good role models, and a prayer plan; and do everything with love. When you are in the storm, know that God has a special plan for you. He will use that storm to strengthen you for your own good, equip you for what is to come, and get you ready for an extraordinary destiny. Let seeing others get through storms empower you and remind you that you too can make it through. The things we go through serve a greater purpose than just our own. Let them help someone else as well.

You must pray, believe, and have faith. The clouds will move on, and the storm you once thought would take you under and out will be over. Persevere and help your sister along the way. While you may be helping your sisters—pouring love into others, empowering other women, and trying to live your best life—it is easy to become enervated or tired. When this happens, refer to the book of Galatians, where it says, "Let us not become weary in doing good, for at the proper time we will reap a harvest if we do not give up" (Galatians 6:9). Good things take time to prosper, so have patience and don't give up.

Refrain from bashing other women, and be there to lend a helping hand instead. If you are not in a position to assist or give advice to someone who is in need, then it is OK to say so. Let them know you aren't able to give them the help they are searching for and direct them to someone who can, if possible. You must first have yourself in order before you can help the next woman. Take the time to become the best version of yourself so you can help empower your sisters later.

Every day, someone is experiencing a storm. If it isn't your season to go through tests and trials, then it is someone else's. Storms are inevitable, so always be kind. Know that life is not easy and it will not get easy. But when you walk in God's shadow, you'll never have to worry about handling it alone. He'll be there to pick you up when you fall every time.

Don't allow life's storms to separate you from your true self. Have a forgiving spirit and love in your heart, and be strong enough to choose you. Your peace is never worth losing. Protect it as if it were a prize. Know when to fight for something you want and when to move on. Have integrity and respect for yourself as well as others. Lastly, be proactive. When the storms appear to be coming your way, stand tall and tell yourself that you are stronger than any storm. Don't let the storms that rage against you defeat you. Walk with God, and he'll be sure to get you through!

# Resources to Help You Face Your Storm

No Matter What
Your Storm May Be,
Know That You
Can Overcome It

Addiction · Abortion · Fear of Rejection · Guilt · Poverty · Hurt · Grief · Hate · Homosexuality · Peer Pressure · Disease · Adultery · Neglect · Physical Abuse · Racism · Anxiety · Unforgiveness · Shame · Denial · Depression · Sorrow · Doubt · Trust Issues · Anger · Fear · Weakness · Jam Pai... · Pain · Lust · Fornication · Suicidal Thoughts · Failure · Sickness · Low Self-Esteem · Self-Righteousness · Divorce · Substance Abuse · Disability · Hate · Gossip

## Things *You* Can Do to Empower Women

Organize a sisterhood
Compliment other women
Give back to other women
Be kind
Encourage other women
Pray for other women
Speak to other women
Congratulate other women
Have a listening ear
Lend a helping hand when needed
Become an accountability partner
*Love your sister!*

### The Lord's Prayer

Our father,
who art in heaven,
hallowed be thy Name,
thy kingdom come,
thy will be done,
on earth as it is in heaven.

Give us this day our daily bread.
And forgive us our trespasses,
as we forgive those
who trespass against us.

And lead us not into temptation,
but deliver us from evil.

For thine is the kingdom,
and the power, and the glory,
for ever and ever. Amen.

## Raging Storms

Dear Lord,
Though storms are inevitable,
I'll never fear, because I realize
That heaven is near.
You are my strength, you are my provider,
You are the one who I can confide in.
Your plans
I will follow,
Without worrying
About the troubles
Of tomorrow.
Through the raging storms
And cloudy days,
Give me the strength
To uplift my sister
Along the way.
Hand in hand, I'll trust your plan,
Because without you,
These raging storms,
I'll never get through.

## Important Bible Scriptures to Remember when Facing a Tough Storm

*"I can do all things through Christ who strengthens me." (Philippians 4:13)*

*"God is within her, she will not fail." (Psalm 46:5)*

*"Guard your heart above all else for it determines the course of your life." (Proverbs 4:23)*

*"And the God of all grace, who called you to his glory in Christ, after you have suffered a little while, will himself restore you and make you strong, firm and steadfast." (1 Peter 5:10)*

*"No weapon formed against you shall prosper." (Isaiah 54:17)*

*"Cast all your anxiety on him because he cares for you." (1 Peter 5:7)*

*"More than that, we rejoice in our sufferings, knowing that suffering produces endurance, and endurance produces character, and character produces hope, and hope does not put us to shame, because God's love has been poured into our hearts through the Holy Spirit who has been given to us." (Romans 5:3–5)*

*"And we know that in all things God works for the good of those who love him, who have been called according to his purpose." (Romans 8:28)*

*"Trust in the Lord with all your heart and lean not on your own understanding; in all your ways submit to him and he will make your paths straight." (Proverbs 3:5–6)*

*"Anxiety weighs down the heart, but a kind word cheers it up." (Proverbs 12:25)*

*"Rejoice in hope; be patient in affliction; be persistent in prayer." (Romans 12:12)*

*"So after you have suffered a little while, he will restore, support, and strengthen you, and he will place you on a firm foundation." (1 Peter 5:10)*

*"The Lord himself goes before you and will be with you; he will never leave you nor forsake you. Do not be afraid; do not be discouraged." (Deuteronomy 31:8)*

*"The Lord hears his people when they call to him for help. He rescues them from all their troubles. The Lord is close to the brokenhearted; he rescues those whose spirits are crushed. The righteous person faces many troubles, but the Lord comes to the rescue each time." (Psalm 34:17–19)*

*"We have troubles all around us, but we are not defeated. We do not know what to do, but we do not give up the hope of living. We are persecuted, but God does not leave us. We are hurt sometimes, but we are not destroyed." (2 Corinthians 4:8–9)*

*"Therefore put on the full armor of God, so that when the day of evil comes, you may be able to stand*

*your ground, and after you have done everything to stand. Stand firm then, with the belt of truth buckled around your breastplate of righteousness in place."*
*(Ephesians 6:13–14)*

*"Cast your burden on the Lord, and he will sustain you; he will never permit the righteous to be moved."*
*(Psalm 55:22)*

## About the Author

I grew up the youngest of four in the city of Memphis, Tennessee. I enjoyed being the youngest because I was able to learn what to do and what not to do from all of the mistakes that my older siblings would make. I was nowhere near perfect but always strived to be.

Music was a way out for me. I listened to all types of genres: everything from R&B, gospel, hip-hop, country, old-school classics—the list goes on. Music seemed to have the answer to every problem. My love for music even included playing musical instruments. I can play the saxophone and clarinet, and I have an eager mind to learn guitar as well.

When I went off to college, I decided to put my musical talents aside and focus on school. I attended

Middle Tennessee State University and obtained a degree in mass communication. Learning to communicate with people and inspire and motivate others is what I appreciate the most about the experience.

Having the opportunity to make a difference in other people's lives brings me great joy. I have a heart for helping people and giving back. One of my favorite scriptures is Philippians 4:13: "I can do all things through Christ who strengthens me" because throughout my life, I've been able to do just that.

*Prayers*

Date: _____

_____
_____
_____
_____
_____
_____
_____
_____
_____
_____
_____
_____

*Answered Prayers*

Date: _____

_____
_____
_____
_____
_____
_____
_____
_____
_____
_____
_____

## Notes